I am in Park Street.
I am going to school.

I am in school.

I am a bus driver.
I am going to Hill Street.

my bus is a big bus.
it is at the bus stop.

I am in school.

I am in the police car and I am going to the park.

the police car is
a big car.

the driver is
a policewoman.

I am a milkman.

I am going
to Park Street School.

my lorry is a little lorry
and I am the driver.

I met
a big policeman today.

the policeman
was reading a paper.

the policeman was going
into the bus.

the bus was going
to Park Street.

I met a lorry driver today.

the lorry driver was
at the bus stop.

the lorry driver
was reading the name
on the bus.

the bus was going
to Hill Street.

I met a bus driver today.

the bus was
at the bus stop.

the driver was going
into the bus
and the bus was going
to the big school.

I met my teacher today.

my teacher was
in the paper shop.

my teacher was reading the name on a paper.

I was reading my comic.

15

I am reading to my teacher
and the bus driver
and the lorry driver
and the policeman
and the milkman.

I am good at reading.